M000042300

PRESENTED TO:

_____

BY:

_____

DATE:

_____

101 SIMPLE SECRETS

TO KEEP YOUR

FAITH ALIVE

HONOR HB BOOKS

Inspiration and Motivation for the Season of Life

An Imprint of Cook Communications Ministries • Colorado Springs, CO

Unless otherwise indicated, all Scripture quotations are taken from the *Holy Bible, New International Version®*. NIV ®. Copyright © 1973, 1978, 1984 by International Bible Society. Used by permission of Zondervan Publishing House. All rights reserved.

All Scripture quotations marked KJV are taken from the *King James Version* of the Bible.

Scripture quotations marked THE MESSAGE are taken from *The Message,* copyright © by Eugene H. Peterson, 1993, 1994, 1995, 1996. Used by permission of NavPress Publishing Group.

Scripture quotations marked NRSV are from the *New Revised Standard Version* of the Bible, copyright © 1989 by The Division of Christian Education of the National Council of the Churches of Christ in the USA. Used by permission. All rights reserved.

All Scripture quotations marked NASB are taken from the *New American Standard Bible.* Copyright © The Lockman Foundation 1960, 1962, 1963, 1968, 1971, 1972, 1973, 1975, 1977, 1995. Used by permission.

08 07 06 05 04   10 9 8 7 6 5 4 3 2 1

101 Simple Secrets to Keep Your Faith Alive
ISBN 1-56292-276-9
Copyright © 2004 by Bordon Books
An Imprint of Cook Communications Ministry
4050 Lee Vance View
Colorado Springs, Colorado 89018

Developed by Bordon Books.

Manuscript compiled by Betsy Williams, Tulsa, Oklahoma, in conjuction with Bordon Books.

Printed in the United States of America. All rights reserved under International Copyright Law. Contents and/or cover may not be reproduced in whole or in part in any form without the express written consent of the Publisher.

INTRODUCTION

In the hectic rush of our everyday lives, our faith can be overlooked and our spiritual growth stunted. What better way to feed your faith and develop your spiritual muscles than to read a book filled with 101 ways to focus your faith, to keep your thoughts positive, and to increase your trust in God's desire to see you succeed. In *101 Simple Secrets to Keep Your Faith Alive*, every two pages are filled with a simple secret, a quotation or scripture, and a faith-building reflection to give you quick and easy ideas for strengthening your faith and helping you draw near to God. You will be surprised by how easy it is to commune with your Creator when you begin to renew your sense of His love for you and His purpose for your life. Begin to grow closer to God today. He is waiting with open arms.

1

BE ON THE LOOKOUT FOR MIRACLES.

---

he whole crowd of disciples began

joyfully to praise God

in loud voices for all the

miracles they had seen.

LUKE 19:37

Does God part seas anymore? Or feed people with manna from Heaven? Maybe you haven't witnessed a miracle of biblical proportions recently. But then again, maybe you haven't had your eyes open wide enough to see the spectacular, as well as the simple but amazing acts of God that are right in front of you.

Perhaps you already know this firsthand. After all, it is a miracle when a person's life—when your life—is changed because of a brand-new response to God's love.

So open your eyes and heart to God's miracles. Expect them, want them, and enjoy them when they occur. *When,* not *if.* As you grow closer to God, your life will be nothing short of miraculous.

MIRACLES TEND TO HAPPEN
TO THOSE WHOSE EYES
ARE OPEN TO SEE THEM.

2

STRIVE FOR A *PERSONAL* RELATIONSHIP WITH GOD.

hat is His call to us—simply to be people who are content to live close to Him and to renew the kind of life in which the closeness is felt and experienced.

There is a big difference between knowing *about* God and truly knowing Him, personally and directly. Take time to be still in God's presence, and ask Him to fill your mind and your heart with His love and wisdom. Books, sermons, and music can all help you experience God's presence, but they should serve only as pathways to God, not destinations unto themselves.

You can't read a movie review, for example, and get the same experience as seeing the movie yourself. And you can't truly understand a place on the globe by poring over a travel brochure. You must go to the place and enjoy it firsthand. God, too, is a personal experience in faith.

YOUR RELATIONSHIP WITH GOD IS ONE THING YOU SHOULD TAKE PERSONALLY.

3

ADMIT WHEN YOU'RE WRONG.

---

*If we confess our sins, he is faithful and
just and will forgive us our sins
and purify us from all unrighteousness.*

1 JOHN 1:9

No one likes to admit when they have done wrong. And yet, when we confess our mistakes to God and to those we have hurt or offended, we are, in a sense, admitting that we are not perfect and that we need God's grace in our lives. Sometimes it is difficult to admit we need God's grace. Without it we can never know the sweet comfort of collapsing into God's arms and hearing Him say, "I forgive you."

Refuse to allow pride and denial to limit your possibilities. God is wise and good. Clear away all that might keep you from knowing Him fully. By being honest with God, you will keep your faith alive.

THERE IS NO PLEA BARGAINING WITH GOD.

4

STOP AND SMELL THE ROSES.

God held my life and your life like flowers in His hand.

"Stop and smell the roses" is a familiar saying. Have you ever stopped and really examined one? The next chance you get, take a long, hard look at one of God's beautiful roses. Note the texture of the petals, the scent, the color. Look deep inside the petals at the stamen. God meticulously crafted even the parts that don't show. Then think of how many varieties of roses there are. The list is endless.

Now think about yourself for a moment. Think about how carefully God knit you together in your mother's womb. Just as no two roses are exactly alike, there is only one you in all the world. Just as you take delight in a beautiful rose, God takes delight in you, His child. Hold that thought, and your faith will grow stronger.

ROSES ARE WONDERFUL, BUT YOU ARE AMAZING!

5

SET YOUR "PET GRUDGE" FREE.

Rid yourselves of all malice.

1 Peter 2:1

Maybe that "pet grudge" was cute when you first got it, but not anymore. It has grown big, demanding, and ugly. Its whining and complaining annoy you and those around you. And it keeps leaving those unsightly stains on your soul. So, it's time to set the grudge free. After all, God says that we must not be resentful (2 Timothy 2:24).

Open your heart's door and shoo the grudge away. Then forgive the person who prompted you to take it in the first place. You will feel better. Your heart will feel lighter. And if that grudge ever comes back and scratches at your door, pretend you're not home. You will then be able to spread your wings of faith into new areas, once blocked by that huge "pet" standing in your way.

THOSE WHO HOLD GRUDGES AREN'T ABLE TO HOLD ON TO GOD—OR MUCH OF ANYTHING ELSE.

6

EXERCISE YOUR RIGHT TO WRITE IN YOUR BIBLE.

If you are serious about your faith, put it in writing.

Reading the Bible should be an interactive experience. As you read, think about how to apply God's words to your life. Write down action steps you plan to take. Underline passages you want to memorize. Highlight portions that confuse you and remind yourself to ask someone about them. The power of God's words does not reside in the impressive leather binding or the gilded edges of the pages, but in their ability to sink into your thoughts and soul.

If you still feel awkward about marking up your Bible, buy a notebook and use it to chronicle your thoughts and responses to God's life-instruction manual written just for you. The Bible is a personal love letter written to help you keep your faith alive.

TO GET THE MOST OUT OF STUDYING THE BIBLE, YOU NEED THE *WRITE* STUFF!

7

AVOID BEING A PEW POTATO.

It's great to have your feet
on the ground,
but keep them moving.

Are you a pew potato? A religious russet? A spiritual spud? Do you merely sit in church week after week, letting the messages and music slide through your ears without making an impression on your brain or your heart?

If so, it's time for a change. Next Sunday, actively *listen* to your pastor's words. Think about how you can apply them to your life—immediately. If the pastor brings up an issue you are struggling with, ask for forgiveness right away. If you are reminded of the struggles of a family member or friend, make a note to pray for that person or write a letter of encouragement. The point is: do something, anything. Don't just sit there; activate your faith.

BEING A PEW POTATO
LEADS TO A HALF-BAKED
SPIRITUAL LIFE.

8

LET GO OF THE PAST.

"*Forget the former things; do not dwell on the past.*
See, I am doing a new thing!"

ISAIAH 43:18-19

No amount of energy can change the past. But holding on to yesterday can rob you of energy you need to handle today. Try to see the upside of past mistakes or misfortune by treating them as colorful material for your life story—motivators that helped you move in new directions.

Of course, there may be some areas of pain and regret that you won't be able to deal with alone. In that case, talk to a counselor or close friend. And don't hesitate to ask for God's help. He's a great listener. Just opening up about what's holding you back can help you put the past where it belongs—in the past. It will open new doors to your future and revitalize your faith.

A REARVIEW MIRROR IS FOR BACKING UP, NOT MOVING FORWARD.

9

LIVE IN THE PRESENT.

" *o not worry about tomorrow,
for tomorrow will
worry about itself. Each day has
enough trouble of its own.*"

MATTHEW 6:34

Are you stressed out today by worrying about what's coming tomorrow? Maybe it's a dental appointment or an important presentation at work. Maybe it's anticipating a doctor's call regarding the results of a medical test. Maybe it's the fear of retirement or the end of a relationship.

Today's stress could even be about something positive such as preparing for vacation, a possible promotion, or working long hours now for a payoff later. But your body was designed to handle only one day at a time. Worry acts like a magnifying glass—everything starts to look bigger than it really is. Putting tomorrow in God's hands and doing what you can today is the best way to wipe out worry. Worry can rob you of your faith. Let it go, and trust God to bring exactly what you need at the moment you need it. This is not easy, so ask God to help you trust Him.

THE PRESENT TIME IS THE TIME TO BE PRESENT.

10

BE ALERT FOR THE "SMALL MIRACLES" THAT HAPPEN EVERY DAY.

To me every hour of the light and dark is a miracle, every cubic inch of space is a miracle.

Miracles happen all around us every day, so often that we routinely overlook them in the moment. It may be hours later that we realize God's miraculous protection surrounded us. It may be only upon quiet reflection that we recognize that being on time for an appointment, despite numerous detours or finding a person in a crowd, had a truly miraculous element to it.

Sometimes the miracles around you are as simple as a bud bursting into bloom or the hatching of birds' eggs outside your kitchen window. Taking time to *see* and appreciate the miraculous is guaranteed to bring a smile to your soul, happiness to your heart, and strength to your faith.

MIRACLES ARE YOURS
FOR THE SEEING.

11

PRAY THE LORD'S PRAYER EVERY DAY.

"Our Father in heaven, hallowed be your name, your kingdom come, your will be done on earth as it is in heaven. Give us today our daily bread. Forgive us our debts, as we also have forgiven our debtors. And lead us not into temptation, but deliver us from the evil one."

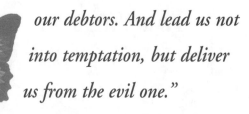

MATTHEW 6:9-13

Prayer is a faith connector and a faith activator. So great is God's love for us that He even taught us what to pray. So on those days when you're not sure what to say to your Father, open up your Bible and follow Jesus' model. Better yet, memorize this prayer (if you haven't already).

However, be careful that you don't let the words become rote, ritualized, and meaningless. After every few words you pray, think about what they mean. Ask yourself, *Did I truly mean what I just said?* If the answer is no, pray the words again. Another way to keep the Lord's Prayer fresh and vibrant in your life is to read or memorize it in several different Bible versions.

THE LORD GAVE YOU HIS PRAYER TO MAKE YOUR OWN.

12

START THE DAY BY READING THE BIBLE.

---

our word is a lamp to my feet and a light for my path.

PSALM 119:105

"Eat a good breakfast," your mom used to say. Good nutrition in the morning imparts energy and strength for the entire day. That's the case with your spiritual energy and strength as well. The Bible is the best source of spiritual nutrition. Its living words can set the course for the whole day when you make it your main focus in the morning.

As you begin, ask God to give you revelation of, or supernatural insight into, the passages you read. Ask Him how you can apply the words to your life that day. If a certain verse stands out to you, jot it down on an index card, and post it where you will see it during the day. It will be a lamp to your feet and a light for your path, wherever your path may take you. A good spiritual breakfast builds strong faith muscles.

A DAY WITHOUT GOD'S WORD IS A DAY WITHOUT SONSHINE.

13

HOLD A BABY IN YOUR ARMS.

God's gifts put man's best dreams to shame.

When people think of God, they tend to think of the Red Sea-parting, burning-in-the-bush God. Awesome power is certainly part of who He is. But God also revealed himself in the form of a helpless baby, born in a manger two thousand years ago. So the next time you hold a baby in your arms, imagine the Ruler of the Universe crying in hunger or needing a nap.

God could have come to Earth as a full-grown, powerful man or a superhuman hero. But when He came as a baby and grew into adulthood, He gave us an opportunity to see faith in action. He deliberately chose a more difficult, humble road—a road that would be like the one we walk. As a result, He knows our experiences, our needs, our emotions, our humanity. Thinking of God as a human who experienced what you are experiencing can make it easier for you to go to Him with your needs and concerns.

THANKS TO GOD'S GREAT LOVE,
WE NEED NEVER SAY,
"BUT YOU DON'T KNOW
WHAT IT'S LIKE DOWN HERE."

14

FORGIVE YOURSELF.

---

*et us draw near to God . . . in full
assurance of faith,
having our hearts sprinkled
to cleanse us from
a guilty conscience.*

HEBREWS 10:22

Guilt is a heavy load to carry, not only emotionally, but also physically. It may be well-earned or just a lifelong accumulation of "should haves." Whatever the source, it's an invisible stressor that won't loose its grip on you until you give up your hold on it. Not only that, it hinders your faith and keeps you from drawing close to God.

Begin by determining where your guilt comes from. Is what you're hearing the truth? Is there something you should do, confess, make up for? If so, take care of it. If your guilt is based on unfounded words of condemnation placed on you by someone in your past, then relief will come only when you recognize and discard them. God has already promised His forgiveness. What's holding you back from forgiving yourself? Finding the answer to that will free you to grow an even stronger faith.

A GUILT TRIP IS
NO VACATION.

15

BREAK INTO SONG.

Sing to the LORD a new song;

sing to the LORD,

all the earth.

PSALM 96:1

Deep at the core of every human being, God has placed the joy of song. This seems to be intended to counterbalance the more routine and troublesome aspects of life and often serves to keep your faith alive. Even if you can't carry a tune in a bucket, releasing that urge to burst forth in song can leave you feeling renewed and invigorated. In fact, singing is often so energizing that individuals have trouble keeping their feet from tapping and their legs from springing forth into dance.

It doesn't have to be any particular song. If you'll just start humming, a "new song" may bubble up from within. Set your heart free—sing for joy!

SING TO THE LORD.
HE LOVES YOUR VOICE.

16

SMILE THE MOMENT YOU
WAKE UP IN THE MORNING.

The more you are thankful
for what you have,
the more you have to be thankful for.

Life with God is something to smile about. Set the tone for the day by smiling as soon as you wake up. First, smile at God, saying in your heart, *Thank You for watching over me all night.* Next, smile at the remembrance of at least one good thing that happened the day before. Then, smile at the thought of all the opportunities and blessings that await you for the upcoming day. Smile at the thought that God will be present throughout the day to help you with every crisis, challenge, or obstacle. Smile because you are alive.

It's hard to be down in the dumps if you have a smile on your face, and smiling is contagious. Try smiling at the various people who come across your face today. You'll feel better, and you will make their day brighter as well.

FAITH HAS A SMILE
ON ITS FACE.

17

PRACTICE MORE WALK, LESS TALK.

---

*G*o unto all the world and
preach the Gospel.
Use words if necessary.

A recent newspaper feature told of an episode of "road rage." The driver of a compact car cut in front of a pickup truck during rush hour. The pickup driver honked at the compact and hollered a few angry words. The compact driver screamed back, made an obscene gesture, and sped away. The noteworthy part of this story is that the compact car was tattooed with Christian bumper stickers, including one that read, "WHAT WOULD JESUS DO?"

It's one thing to talk about how you are drawing closer to God or to proclaim it with stickers and posters. It's another matter to live as God would want you to, even in the heat of rush hour. There are special promises to those who walk the walk, promises whose answers will boost your faith.

A GOOD EXAMPLE IS
THE BEST SERMON.

18

BE PROUD OF HIM.

"*Whoever acknowledges me before men,
I will also acknowledge him
before my Father in heaven.
But whoever disowns me before men,
I will disown him before
my Father in heaven.*"

MATTHEW 10:32-33

We are proud of our children, our yards, our cars, our achievements. We are eager to display them to others and to extol their many fine qualities. But it's sometimes a different story with God. Sometimes we are afraid to identify ourselves as His children because we fear we will be criticized—or labeled as religious fanatics.

The next time you feel a sense of embarrassment over your desire to grow closer to God, ask yourself, *What do I have to be ashamed of?* And ask God to help you to understand His greatness. After all, God is creative and powerful. He is loving. He is merciful. He is the perfect Father. So why wouldn't we be the proudest offspring in the world? And being proud of God is part of a vital, growing faith.

YOU CAN'T BE CLOSE TO HIM ON THE INSIDE IF YOU ARE AFRAID TO ACKNOWLEDGE HIM ON THE OUTSIDE.

19

PRACTICE PATIENCE.

One moment of patience may ward off great disaster.

Patience is part of God's character. If you want to grow closer to Him, you must cultivate and nourish it in your life. So the next time you're stuck in traffic or in a long, slow-moving supermarket line, say to yourself, *I'm not going to let this situation get to me. I'm going to practice patience.* Then use the time to pray for someone—how about the person who is testing your patience?

Practicing patience with people and situations will help you better appreciate how patient God is with your own imperfections and mistakes. It will cause your faith to grow, and you will begin to feel closer to Him.

PRACTICE PATIENCE OFTEN.
PRACTICE MAKES PERFECT.

20

PUT AWAY THE SUPERMAN (OR SUPERWOMAN) CAPE.

*Faith does nothing alone—
nothing of itself, but
everything under God,
by God, through God.*

Have you noticed how none of the TV or comic-book super-heroes ever pray or go to church? Perhaps these individuals feel they don't need God. For us mortals, however, it's a different story. When you try to be a superhero and tackle life with your own human powers, you weaken your relationship with God. After all, faith comes from trusting that He is great enough to help you with the big things and also the little things in life.

Why would trying to take care of yourself weaken your faith? Because only when you admit you are weak can you experience His strength. Only when you acknowledge that you are sick can you know His healing. Only when you realize that you need His help can you receive the help you need. So put your spirit of independence aside, and let Him meet your need. Your faith in Him will grow by leaps and bounds.

PUT AWAY THAT SUPERHERO CAPE. IT DOESN'T GO WITH WHAT YOU'RE WEARING.

21

COUNT YOUR BLESSINGS.

---

*From the fullness of his grace
we have all received
one blessing after another.*

JOHN 1:16

A child living in a third-world country wrote a letter to his American sponsor describing how his home had been flooded by recent storms. "The good news," he wrote, "is at least now we have fish!" There is good to be found in even the most difficult situations. Taking time, not only to notice your blessings, but also to savor them, helps you keep things in perspective.

What are you thankful for today? Why not take some time each morning to consider that question. Then take your answer to God with a heart full of gratitude and praise. When you bring His faithfulness to the forefront, it increases your faith for the future. What better way could there be to begin your day?

A THANKFUL HEART
IS A HAPPY HEART.

22

TAKE GOD AT HIS WORD.

You know with all your heart . . .
that not one of all the
good promises the LORD
your God gave you has failed.

JOSHUA 23:14

Having someone you can trust, no matter what, is like finding a safe house in a hostile world. Even a committed spouse or well-intentioned friend may make promises they can't keep. They cannot guarantee they'll always be there or even always understand.

But God can! He's the only One who has kept every promise He's ever made. That makes Him not only faithful but trust-worthy. When life is at its most stressful, relying on God's promises is a secure and relaxing respite from the storm. God has promised to be with you always, to hear your prayers, to forgive you, and to love you unconditionally. Those are promises you can depend on.

TO TAKE GOD AT HIS WORD, YOU FIRST NEED TO KNOW WHAT HE'S SAYING.

23

STARE AT A STAR.

*He determines the number
of the stars and
calls them each by name.*

PSALM 147:4

Life is bigger than your to-do list. But it's easy to lose perspective when your days are spent running from one appointment to the next, putting out one fire after another, and always feeling as though you're lagging just a bit behind the Joneses.

Stop—even if just for a moment. Take a good look at the world around you. Meditate on the mystery of a distant star, the brilliance of a fleeting sunset, the testimony of a spring flower. Then think about the miracle of there being only one you throughout all of eternity. It is liberating to ponder being such a tiny speck in a seemingly limitless universe, and yet being so deeply loved by such a great God.

LIFE IS A GIFT TO BE CELEBRATED, NOT A TASK TO BE TACKLED.

24

DETERMINE TO RESPECT AND OBEY GOD'S RULES OF RIGHT LIVING.

I have hidden your word in my heart that I might not sin against you.

PSALM 119:11

Farmers have a saying that goes, "Once you're standing in the pigpen, it's too late to worry about soiling your Sunday clothes." And that advice carries beyond the farm. How can you grow close to God if you are busy doing those things that hurt Him, hurt you, and hurt others?

God has given us a code of conduct to live by. In the same way you would steer your child away from danger, these injunctions to right living are intended to steer you out of harm's way. Determine right now to resist those things that are contrary to God's rules of right living, and commit to avoid settings in which you'll likely face temptation. Right living not only keeps your faith alive, but the Bible tells us that it also unveils spiritual truths we could see no other way than by the way of obedience.

AN OUNCE OF PREVENTION IS WORTH A POUND OF REPENTENCE

25

HONOR YOUR SPOUSE.

---

*Successful marriage is
always a triangle:
a man, a woman, and God.*

God could have used any number of analogies to illustrate His relationship with His followers: employer/employee, teacher/student, even master/slave. But the one He chose was groom/bride. Clearly, the relationship between husband and wife is important to Him.

So when you praise, compliment, care for, and celebrate your spouse, you honor a relationship God himself created—and you understand better how much God cherishes those who respond to His love and care. If you are single, the Bible says that God himself will look after you as a husband. Direct your praises His way, and you will be, of all, the most blessed.

DIVORCE YOURSELF FROM ANYTHING THAT COMES BETWEEN YOU AND YOUR SPOUSE.

26

DISCOVER GOD'S PURPOSE
FOR YOUR LIFE.

*The purposes of the Almighty are
perfect, and must prevail,
though we erring mortals may fail
to accurately perceive them in advance.*

Do you have a sense of wonder about what you do in life? For example, if you're a teacher, are you merely downloading a bunch of facts into your students' minds or inspiring them with the thrill of learning? Is teaching just a job, or is it a calling?

If what you do is just a job, you may have missed God's purpose for your life. Think of the first disciples Jesus called. They left all that they had to follow Him. Their hearts pounded with anticipation. Yours should as well. God's plan is for you to experience an abundant, vibrant life in perfect harmony with the gifts and callings He has placed in you. Find those, and you will be one step closer to Him and one step closer to keeping your faith alive.

HAPPINESS IS KNOWING WHAT YOU WERE MEANT TO BE.

27

JOIN A BIBLE STUDY GROUP.

tudy to shew thyself approved
unto God, a workman that
needeth not to be ashamed,
rightly dividing the word of truth.

2 TIMOTHY 2:15 KJV

Bible studies are a great way to study the Bible in depth and learn how to apply its lessons to your life. Bible studies may center around a particular book of the Bible or focus on a particular topic. Many times, these gatherings will be mentioned in the weekly bulletin of the sponsoring church. Some studies meet on church grounds, while others meet in homes. The input of others will provide new insights and a fresh perspective, which will help your faith grow.

Another benefit of joining a Bible study is that you can connect with others who share your faith. And when you are going through times of difficulty, the prayer support you receive will help you to keep your faith level high.

STUDYING THE BIBLE WITH OTHERS WILL ENRICH YOUR TIMES OF PRIVATE STUDY.

28

PRACTICE HUMILITY.

---

he fear of the LORD teaches
a man wisdom, and
humility comes before honor.

PROVERBS 15:33

We live in a day in which those with political clout, wealth, beauty, and fame occupy the "Most Admired" lists. However, God's standards are different. Think of Jesus' parables. The last shall be first, and the first last. A small seed becomes a great tree. One lost sheep takes priority over the rest of the flock.

The Bible defines faith as walking humbly before God. And as we walk practicing humility, we become more in tune with the character of a God who left Heaven to become a vulnerable human. We also learn how much God will employ His power for someone who acknowledges their weakness. God understands humility personally. Jesus was so humble that He obeyed God even to the point of a humiliating and painful death—for our sake. And God showed himself powerfully by the glory He gave Jesus upon His resurrection.

THOSE WHO SING THEIR OWN PRAISES USUALLY SING SOLO.

29

FACE FAILURE WITH COURAGE.

The glory is not in never failing,

but in rising

every time you fall.

To fail seems almost un-American. Yet Christopher Columbus' failure to find Asia actually led him to discover America. Failure happens. Even Pepsi-Cola went bankrupt three times before finding its current success. It was even offered for sale to the Coca-Cola Company. Coca-Cola passed.

Just because you've failed doesn't make you a failure. It just makes you human. Fear of failure will not only put your body under additional stress, but it limits your chances for success in the future. You can't succeed without taking risks. There is something to be learned from every endeavor, whether you regard it as a triumph or a turkey. When you try, you stretch your faith. Perhaps it's time to stretch a little.

EVERY FAILURE HOLDS
THE SEEDS OF SUCCESS.

30

CRY YOUR HEART OUT.

*Tears are often the telescope
by which men
see far into heaven.*

The shortest verse in the Bible is, "Jesus wept" (John 11:35). Jesus' tears were over the death of a friend—someone whom Jesus knew He would momentarily raise from the dead. But still, He wept.

There are things in this life worth crying over. Even God acknowledges that. Psalm 56:8 KJV says God keeps every one of your tears in a bottle. How big is that bottle? Is it a gallon jug or vial so small it holds hardly a trace of salt? Whatever tears are not released from the eyes are stored in the heart. A heavy heart can hinder your intimacy with God and weigh down your faith. So give yourself permission to let go. God's shoulder is always available.

A TEAR CAN ONLY BE DRIED
ONCE IT'S BEEN CRIED.

31

REMEMBER THAT HE IS
ALWAYS WITH YOU.

Where love is, there is God also.

God cannot be contained in a building or a book. Yet it is easy for us to forget Him unless we are in church or reading the Bible. Sometimes, in the middle of life's daily busyness, we stop communicating with Him. Instead, our attention is on our computer screen, our checkbook, or the cars ahead of us in the traffic jam.

Don't allow life's details to turn your attention from your Creator. In the midst of your labor and duties, come to recognize that God is always right there with you—to hear you and to speak to you. His temple is always as close as your heart, waiting for you to enter and be refreshed and inspired.

GOD IS ALWAYS JUST
A PRAYER AWAY.

32

REST.

Even the best racehorse has to stop for oats once in a while.

God doesn't sweat. He doesn't get tired. He doesn't struggle with aching muscles after a day of hard work. Yet the Bible says that when He finished creating the world, He rested. If our all-powerful God took the time to rest, that should speak volumes to us mere mortals.

You need to rest occasionally. You need to recover physically, emotionally, and spiritually from life's demands. And, in resting, you will find the time and the right frame of mind to contemplate God's wonders and to thank Him for His grace and kindness to you. You will also gather the energy to run the next miles of your journey with Him and toward Him. Rest is what God recommends to recharge your faith.

TO RUN YOUR RACE WITH OPTIMUM EFFICIENCY, YOU MUST KEEP YOUR BATTERIES CHARGED.

33

CONTEMPLATE HEAVEN.

He puts a little of heaven in
our hearts so that
we'll never settle for less.

2 CORINTHIANS 5:5 THE MESSAGE

Some days, you catch a glimpse of Heaven. Perhaps it's the birth of your first child or watching a sunset reflecting on ocean waves. At those times, your heart may whisper, *This is as good as it gets.* But most days your heart says exactly the opposite: *There's got to be more to life!*

What your heart's really saying is, *There's no place like home.* God created us to live a life with Him where there's no more death, tears, mortgages, deadlines, or pain. And God's character suggests that Heaven will be much more like a lively wedding feast with all the joys of life than an endless choir rehearsal. Now that's something to look forward to!

WHEN LIFE GETS YOU DOWN, DON'T FORGET TO LOOK UP.

34

WORK ON MY DEFENSE.

---

lways be prepared to give an

answer to everyone

who asks you to give the reason

for the hope that you have.

1 PETER 3:15

If you were called into court and asked to defend God's existence and purpose, could you do it? Could you craft a compelling case to support your beliefs?

The Bible tells us to be ready to give a thoughtful, reasonable defense for the hope that is in us. So if you want to keep your faith in God alive, it's important to know why you believe that He exists at all and to be able to support it intellectually. In the process of building a strong defense for your faith, you'll become more confident in your own heart and mind that God *does* exist and wants to be personally involved in your life.

KNOWING WHY YOU BELIEVE WHAT YOU BELIEVE HELPS TO SOLIDIFY YOUR FAITH.

35

LET GOD BE GOD.

Pile your troubles on God's shoulders—

he'll carry your load,

he'll help you out.

PSALM 55:22 THE MESSAGE

Being God is quite an endeavor. All-powerful. All knowing. Able to be everywhere at once. Holy. Just. Infallible. He is the essence of love itself. Human beings don't measure up, but that doesn't seem to keep us from trying. Sound familiar? If so, it may be time to practice the art of letting God be God.

As you have probably already discovered, feeling ultimately responsible for your own life and the lives of others can be an incredibly heavy burden—and it's futile. None of us really have much to say about what life brings our way. So make good, informed choices, plan and prepare, work hard—and leave the rest to God. When you let Him do His job, you express your faith in Him and His faithfulness to do His work. It will make your own faith come alive in ways that may surprise you.

GOD DOESN'T EXPECT YOU TO DO HIS JOB.

36

HAVE A CHAT WITH MY
HEAVENLY FATHER.

Certain thoughts are prayers. There are moments when, whatever the attitude of the body, the soul is on its knees.

A car is driving on the wrong side of the road, headed straight for you. What's your first thought? In life-or-death situations, it's often that little voice that yells out, "Oh, God, no!" or "Please, help me!"

Everyone knows how to pray. It's a natural part of life, but too often it's reserved for those moments when you know without a doubt that circumstances are out of your hands.

Why wait until then? Talking over problems with a friend has been shown to restore a sense of well-being. And God is a good and faithful friend—One who actually has the power to help. Share the details of your life with Him. You will find that He cares very deeply about the things that weigh you down. Under the influence of His love, your trust in Him will make you able to give more and more of your life into His care.

GETTING ON YOUR KNEES
HELPS YOU GET BACK
UP ON YOUR FEET.

37

GIVE TO THOSE IN NEED.

o all the good you can,

By all the means you can,

In all the ways you can,

In all the places you can,

At all the times you can,

To all the people you can,

As long as ever you can.

In one of His most compelling messages, Jesus taught that when we help the sick, the poor, the imprisoned, it is the same as doing it for Him. He didn't say that it's *like* we're helping Him. He said, "I tell you the truth, whatever you did for one of the least of these brothers of mine, you did for me" (Matthew 25:40).

When we realize all that Jesus has done for us, we naturally want to bless Him in return. Learning to recognize Him in the hungry faces of third-world children, the hopeless eyes of the street beggar, even the hardened expression of the convict is an important step in keeping our faith alive and developing our relationship with Him. The difficulties in loving the last, the lost, and the least will challenge our faith and make it grow.

WHEN WE BLESS OTHERS, WE BLESS JESUS.

38

EXPLORE THE CHRISTIAN CLASSICS.

*Christian literature has
some best-sellers,
but even more blessed sellers.*

Do you want to be a good parent? Watch and learn from parents who are raising fulfilled, happy children. Want to be a good coach? Find one with a winning record, whose team respects him or her and competes with skill, maturity, and class.

But what about improving your spiritual life and drawing closer to God? One way to accomplish this goal is to read the Christian classics. People like George MacDonald, Hannah Whitall Smith, C.S. Lewis, Madam Guyon, Martin Luther, and Charles Sheldon have honestly and eloquently written about many areas of Christian life and the challenges to growing closer to God. Their wisdom and inspiration are sure to strengthen your faith and are only a trip to the bookstore or library away.

GLEAN FROM THOSE
WHO HAVE EXCELLED IN
THEIR WALK WITH GOD:
READ THE CLASSICS.

39

REMEMBER TO SAY, "THANK YOU!"

Thanks be to God
for his
indescribable gift!

2 CORINTHIANS 9:15

Thanksgiving Day has been set aside as a time to thank God for blessings. But if you are serious about keeping your faith alive, you shouldn't wait until you are gnawing on a turkey leg or stuffing yourself with dressing to thank God for all He has done.

Whenever you feel God's hand on your life, let Him know. When you see Him working in the lives of those around you, thank Him for that too. And don't worry if you're sometimes unsure of how to express your deep gratitude for His goodness. Just thank Him like you would thank anyone else. He'll get the message. After all, He's God.

SHOWING APPRECIATION IS A GREAT WAY TO DEVELOP INTIMACY WITH GOD.

40

LAUGH MORE.

---

*I believe God loves to hear
His children laugh.
What healthy father doesn't?*

If you are a parent, grandparent, or around children very often, you know the pure joy that comes from hearing a child's laughter—especially if you had something to do with inspiring it. God has given us the gift of laughter not only as a way to nourish our souls but also as an expression of our faith in Him. The Bible records that "When the righteous see God in action they'll laugh, they'll sing, they'll laugh and sing for joy" (Psalm 68:3 THE MESSAGE). In Psalm 100:2 THE MESSAGE, we are told to "Bring a gift of laughter, sing yourselves into his [God's] presence."

God loves it when we laugh. So the next time you witness a humous incident or hear a funny story or joke, don't rein in your laughter. And when you hear of God's work of love in someone's life, unleash it. Chances are, God is smiling, or even laughing, right along with you.

LAUGHTER ADDS SPICE TO ANY RELATIONSHIP. TRY SHARING YOUR LAUGHTER WITH GOD.

41

LOVE YOUR ENEMIES.

"*You have heard that it was said, 'Love your neighbor and hate your enemy.' But I tell you: Love your enemies and pray for those who persecute you.*"

MATTHEW 5:43-44

Is there any tougher commandment than to love our enemies? We are not to simply tolerate them or do kind things for them, but we are told to love them.

Those obnoxious, cruel, hateful people? Yeah, right!, you think to yourself.

Yes, that is right, and the first step to loving your enemies is to pray for them (not for their humiliation or destruction, by the way). And when you pray for your enemies, pray also for your own negative attitude toward their behavior. Sincerely apply your faith. You certainly don't need bitterness toward others to stand between the relationship you have with God!

As you experience what hard work it is to love unlovable people, you will gain new respect for the fact that while you were yet a sinner, Christ died for you (Romans 5:8). That's very good news. But the joy you experience when you find that kind of love flowing out of you from God is even better news.

YOU ARE NO LONGER GOD'S ENEMY. YOU ARE HIS FRIEND.

42

LOVE THE UNLOVABLE.

"*They say, 'Here is a glutton and a drunkard, a friend of tax collectors and "sinners."' But wisdom is proved right by her actions.*"

MATTHEW 11:19

In Jesus' time, Jews were legally forbidden to associate with the likes of beggars, tax collectors, and prostitutes. So when He befriended such people, Jesus didn't merely smash social and cultural barriers, He broke Jewish law. And He didn't just spout scriptures to these people. He hung out with them. He ate with them, and He touched them.

That's why it's so important to remember that the homeless, drunks, and derelicts you encounter are loved by God as much as you are. And how you respond to them, how you treat them, is a reflection of your relationship with the Heavenly Father. In loving the last, the lost, and the least, you will get to know God and to trust Him in ways you hadn't anticipated.

HOW WE TREAT THE DOWNTRODDEN AND OUTCASTS WE ENCOUNTER IS HOW WE TREAT THE FATHER.

43

SLOW DOWN TO PRAY.

*If you haven't got the time
to talk to God,
you don't have a prayer.*

Are your prayers quick monologues *to* God or conversations *with* God? Prayer is as much about listening to Him as it is about speaking to Him. Often we hit God with a barrage of requests, utter a few halfhearted thank-you's, then hurry on to the next order of the day. That is not prayer.

Like conversation with a friend, true prayer is unhurried. It's communication with your Heavenly Father, the Creator of the Universe. So slow down. Enter His presence in quietness and reverence. Pay attention to the words and feelings you get from Him as you pray. And let your prayers take as long as they need to take. Focus on communication rather than agendas, schedules, or limits. You'll see your faith come alive every time.

THE BIRDS THAT FLY HIGHEST ARE THE BIRDS OF "PRAY."

44

REALIZE THAT INTIMACY
WITH GOD TAKES TIME.

---

*esus grew in wisdom and stature, and
in favor with God and men.*

LUKE 2:52

We live in an age of immediate gratification with its instant coffee, instant rice, and microwave popcorn. Even first-class mail is now "snail mail." We must realize that there is no instant formula for obtaining intimacy with God. Some have sought a shortcut, only to give up in discouragement.

Relationships take time. And the very idea of growing closer to God denotes a process: learning more about Him, growing more aware of His presence in your life, becoming more confident in His love for you, and exercising your faith in His faithfulness to keep His promises. So take the time to get to know God. You'll be glad you did.

GROWING IN YOUR PERSONAL RELATIONSHIP WITH GOD IS A MARATHON, NOT A FORTY-YARD DASH.

45

STRIVE TO BE A SAINT, NOT A CELEBRITY.

"Whoever exalts himself will be humbled, and whoever humbles himself will be exalted."

MATTHEW 23:12

To some, life is a theater in which they play the role of celebrity. They flaunt their talents and accomplishments, even their superspirituality. They are like the Pharisees of Jesus' day, who made a big production even out of fasting. They wanted everyone to be impressed by their long, hungry faces.

It is human nature to do this in one way or another, to hide behind masks that cloak insecurities or selfish agendas. The walk of faith is no place for masks, however. It's a place for bare faces, blemishes and all. It is a place where people look each other in the eye and look to God for guidance, hope, and forgiveness. Does that seem impossible? All things are possible with God. Ask Him to help you be an honest saint and give up any masks you've been wearing.

THE WORLD HAS ENOUGH CELEBRITIES. IT COULD USE A FEW MORE SAINTS.

46

DON'T WORRY. BE HAPPY.

*"Who of you by worrying can add
a single hour to his life?"*

MATTHEW 6:27

It's amazing how worrying about things can take our eyes off God. And there are plenty of things in this earthly life that we could worry about: finances, our children, our jobs, the future, and terrorism. However, worrying about matters doesn't change anything, and it ties our insides up in knots.

At times like these, you must step back and regain perspective. It is vital to focus on the fact that you are greatly and eternally loved by the Almighty God. Then, give your worries to Him in prayer and *leave* them there. If you find that difficult to do, remember that you are entrusting your cares to the One who hung the stars and set the planets into motion, the One who created the earth and all that is in it. He is more than able to handle even your most troubling worry, and He's eager to do so. Trust Him with your worries, and watch your faith grow as He shows you just how dependable He can be.

WORRY IS THE INTEREST PAID BY THOSE WHO BORROW TROUBLE.

47

COME NEAR TO HIM.

Submit yourselves, then, to God. . . .

Come near to God and

he will come near to you.

JAMES 4:7-8

To be near God, you don't have to be perfect. But there is one requirement: you must totally submit yourself to Him. That means nothing held back—unconditional surrender. Just as you can't be "mostly married" or "somewhat pregnant," you cannot think of God as a "nodding acquaintance." A relationship with Him simply doesn't work that way.

If you choose to hang on to some area of your life, will God still love you? Of course! He loved you long before you were even aware of Him. But if you truly want to grow close to God, to know Him as a friend, to grow in your trust in Him, you must give yourself completely to Him with nothing held back.

TO BE HOLY, YOU MUST BE WHOLLY HIS.

48

OPEN YOUR HEART.

"Here I am! I stand at the door and knock.

If anyone hears my voice

and opens the door,

I will come in and eat with him,

and he with me."

REVELATION 3:20

Life's pain and disappointment can batter our faith and cause us to close our hearts tight like a fist. Or we may close our hearts to hold on to something we fear losing. Unfortunately, a tense heart can't relax, can't laugh, can't truly love—and it can't fully receive God's love.

An open heart signals a readiness for whatever changes, surprises, and gifts God has to offer. It is alive in faith. Picture your heart as a door—a door that you can leave open for God. After all, He is the One who built the door and the house. And He has already made it clear that He wants to come in and stay with you forever. Take a first step on the road to an open heart by asking God to help you trust Him and open up to Him.

A HEART OPEN TO GOD IS
A HEART OPEN TO GOOD.

49

TRAVEL LIGHT.

Whoever loves money never
has money enough;
whoever loves wealth is never
satisfied with his income.

ECCLESIASTES 5:10

Many Americans have a possession obsession—every conceivable electronic gizmo, expensive jewelry, elaborate homes, sports cars. These items aren't inherently bad, but they can easily become sources of security and even pride.

Jesus taught His followers to travel light, to take with them only what they would need for their journey. Only the mind set on things above will have a life of peace and faith, so refuse to become distracted by the glitter of shiny things. Why? Because the light of God's divine love is so brilliant that it makes everything else pale in comparison. If you want to really know Him, don't get distracted by worldly possessions. Place your focus where you are going to be the longest—in eternity with Him.

THE EXCESS BAGGAGE OF MATERIALISM ALWAYS MAKES THE JOURNEY MORE DIFFICULT.

50

REMEMBER THAT IT PAYS TO PRAISE.

Doth not all nature around me praise God? If I were silent, I should be an exception to the universe.

One of the Bible's most reassuring promises is found in Psalm 22:3, which says that God inhabits the praise of His people. This is a rather mysterious concept, but we can be confident that when we praise God, when we commend Him, when we express our esteem for Him, somehow His presence is there.

So come closer to God. Adore Him. Thank Him. Praise Him. Celebrate Him. Worship Him in whatever way best expresses what's in your heart. Talk to Him. Sing to Him. Or lift your eyes toward Heaven and simply smile at Him. He will be there with you. And realize that, when you praise God, your faith comes alive and grows in surprising ways. You are not stroking a gigantic ego when you praise—you are acknowledging the truth; and when you do, that truth begins to change you from the inside out and increases your trust in Him.

ENJOYING YOUR PRAISE
IS ONE OF GOD'S
FAVORITE PLACES TO BE.

51

KEEP A SPIRITUAL JOURNAL.

The only important thing a writer needs is a subject.

Your relationship with God is worth writing home about. Record your thoughts, discoveries, applications, questions, goals. Putting these things in writing helps make them more tangible— and easier to remember. Another benefit of the spiritual journal is that you can look back on it and note the progress you've made in your journey with God. This will motivate you and keep your faith alive. You can see how He's made clear what once was confusing. And you can recall how He has answered your prayers.

During those times when God seems far away and you are having difficulty connecting with Him, your spiritual journal can act as a letter written to God. After all, letter writing is an age-old, treasured form of communication. You can believe God will read it, and it will never be marked "Return to sender."

YOUR STORY IS PART
OF HIS STORY.

52

ADMIRE HIS CREATION.

he heavens declare the glory of God; the skies proclaim the work of his hands.

PSALM 19:1

Just as the vision, passion, and talent of a great painter can be seen in his art, God has revealed himself to you through His creation. Allow yourself to be awed and moved by the intricacy, wonder, and beauty of God's handiwork—the expanse of the sky filled with stars, the vastness of the oceans, and the marvel of the human body. As you take it all in, your faith will grow.

And remember, this all-powerful Master Creator loves *you* and wants to have a personal relationship with *you*. He desires it so much that He has painted a magnificent masterpiece in His creation to draw you to His side. So look around the universe, and read His love letter to the world—your name is on the address label!

THE UNIVERSE IS GOD'S WORK OF ART AND WORK OF HEART.

53

DARE TO TRUST HIM.

Trust in him at all times, O people;
pour out your hearts to him,
for God is our refuge.

PSALM 62:8

God is an authority figure, and some of us fear authority figures. We may picture an angry father or a harsh teacher or coach. Perhaps someone like this abused their authority over you, and it wounded you, leaving a deep scar. Now, perhaps, you're afraid to get too close to God. Because of the pain from the past, you're not sure you can ever trust again.

If that is where you find yourself, fear not! God understands, and He will not betray you, disappoint you, or abuse you. He proved His love and faithfulness to you when He, in the person of His Son, willingly died for *you*. Run to Him as your refuge, and find comfort in His loving arms. Give Him a chance to restore your faith.

WHENEVER YOU ARE READY, HIS ARMS ARE OPEN WIDE.

54

HEED HIS CORRECTION.

Whoever heeds correction

is honored.

PROVERBS 13:18

The Bible notes that God reproves those He loves. He isn't out to ruin you or make you pay for something you've done. He simply wants to protect you from the disasters your willfulness could possibly create. How does He correct you? You may hear His voice speaking deep within. A word in Scripture may prick your conscience. Or God may urge someone to speak a word of truth to you. Whatever the avenue, He will be kind. He will never condemn you. If you ignore Him, however, you will most likely suffer the consequences of your actions.

God's reproof is like a mirror, reminding you when your face is dirty and needs washing. Keeping your faith alive requires an honest look inside your heart. And if you see something that needs to be changed or made right, with God's help—do it.

GOD CORRECTS, BUT
HE DOES IT IN LOVE.

55

MEMORIZE A VERSE A WEEK.

I used to have trouble memorizing stuff,
before I read that book
by what's His name.

You probably won't have a Bible at your fingertips every moment of your life. But you can have God's wisdom "at the ready" if you make a commitment to memorize just one verse a week. You may think you're not good at memorizing, but you can probably recite a few key verses already—not to mention the "Pledge of Allegiance" and most of the words to "The Star-Spangled Banner."

As you memorize each verse, think about its implications and how you might apply it in everyday life. Armed with God's Word in your mind and heart, you'll not only keep your faith alive, you'll make it grow. And on top of that you'll begin to make wise choices.

ASK GOD TO HELP YOU RECALL SCRIPTURE, AND DON'T FORGET TO SAY, "THANKS FOR THE MEMORIES."

56

READ CHRISTIAN MAGAZINES.

---

*Finally, brothers, whatever is true,
whatever is noble, whatever is right,
whatever is pure, whatever is lovely,
whatever is admirable—if anything
is excellent or praiseworthy—
think about such things.*

PHILIPPIANS 4:8

If you've passed by a newsstand recently, you've probably noticed the variety of magazines available. Whether you're a scuba diver, chocolate lover, or dirt-bike rider, there's a magazine for you.

But what you may not know is that there are dozens of Christian magazines tailored to a variety of interests. You can read about Christian music, Christian athletes, or Christian media personalities. There are even magazines for worship leaders and biblical archaeology buffs. Take the time to investigate what's available. You'll probably find a publication that addresses your passion for your hobby or area of interest—and your passion for God. Other Christians who share your passion will encourage your own faith to grow as you read what they are learning and writing about.

GOD CAN EVEN USE A MAGAZINE AT THE CHECKOUT TO DRAW YOU TO HIM.

57

AVOID SCREENING GOD'S CALLS.

"He calls his own sheep by name."

JOHN 10:3

We spend much of our lives in front of screens. Computer screens, TV screens, movie screens. Some of your screen time is unavoidable, but think about how much time you can waste in front of various screens. A little channel surfing or Web surfing can subtly turn into hours that leave you with little more than glazed eyes and a couch potato shape.

What's worse, screen time can gobble up hours that could be put to better use—time with God, family, or friends. Time is one of the most valuable possessions you will ever have. Don't waste it. Invest it in things of lasting value, and keep your faith alive by committing to carefully screening your screen time. You don't want busy distractions to cause you to miss out on the spiritual adventures God has in store for you. Leave some time open every day just for the purpose of listening to His messages.

SCREENING OUT GOD'S CALL WILL LEAVE YOU SPIRITUALLY EMPTY.

58

REMEMBER THAT GOD
DID THE CHOOSING.

---

*He [God] chose us in him before
the creation of the world
to be holy and blameless in his sight.*

EPHESIANS 1:4

Remember the thrill of being picked first for a sports team? Or the agony of being picked last—or ending up on a team purely by default? One of the beautiful things about a life in close relationship with God is knowing that each of us has been chosen first for His team.

God chose you long before you chose Him—before you decided that you wanted to be close to Him. In fact, the Bible says that He chose you even before the foundations of the earth were set in place. That's right! God chose you first, and even the little prodding in your heart that makes you want to know Him more comes from Him. You are number one in His eyes. Think about that, and let your faith in Him grow.

IF GOD DIDN'T CHOOSE,
WE'D LOSE.

59

TREAT YOUR BODY LIKE A TEMPLE, NOT A BOWLING ALLEY.

The body is matter, but it is God's creation . . . when it is neglected or scoffed at, God himself is insulted.

If an esteemed guest came to live with you, what accommodations would you provide? Wouldn't you try to make your home as inviting and pleasant as possible? The Bible teaches that our bodies are the temples of God's Spirit. That means that when you made Jesus your Savior and Lord, you invited Him to come and live inside you—as a permanent resident.

Is your temple an appropriate dwelling place for God? You don't have to be a model or an Olympic athlete, but your body is a gift from God. So honor Him by treating it right. Exercize and get enough sleep so that when you spend time with Him you stay awake. Eat foods that keep you alert and able to hear His voice throughout the day. And your mind? Read books, and watch the kinds of films that honor Him and don't make Him uncomfortable.

GUARDING YOUR HEALTH
SHOWS RESPECT FOR
YOUR CREATOR.

60

OBEY THE TEN COMMANDMENTS.

"*ou shall have no other gods before me.*

You shall not make for yourself an idol. . . .

You shall not misuse the name of the LORD
your God. . . .

Remember the Sabbath day by keeping it holy. . . .

Honor your father and your mother. . . .

You shall not murder. You shall not commit adultery.

You shall not steal. You shall not give
false testimony against your neighbor.
You shall not covet."

EXODUS 20:3-5,7-8,12-17

Long before David Letterman, God created the original "Top Ten" list—His Ten Commandments. These rules for right living aren't allowed to be posted in some schools anymore, but they should be inscribed in our hearts and minds. The Ten Commandments are more than wise guidelines for living a holy and pleasing life; they also tell us much about God's passion, what makes His heart beat.

As you follow the Ten Commandments, you walk in step with their author, and His values become your values as well. Soon you will find yourself thinking like He thinks and doing what He would do. You will never know God completely—in many ways He is unknowable. But you can learn to walk by His side and keep in step with Him. The adventures that following Him will bring will be an inspiration to keep your faith alive!

GOD'S COMMANDMENTS
ARE A PERFECT TEN.

61

ENJOY THE BEAUTY OF NATURE.

Apprentice yourself to nature.
Not a day will pass
without her opening a new and
wondrous world of experience
to learn from and enjoy.

God has made some amazing things! Sometimes we become blinded to the beauty of creation because we are so focused in our daily routines. Make a point to get out and reacquaint yourself with God's incomparable creativity. Notice the flowers, trees, birds, and squirrels. Look at the blue sky and the clouds floating by. Take in the sights, sounds, and smells. Think about the kind of person God must be to make this kind of world.

Use this as time to commune with your Heavenly Father. Be sure and tell Him the things you love about His creation. Keep your spiritual ears open as well. As you are taking in the sights and sounds, you may receive fresh revelation from Him that will boost your faith.

WHAT BETTER WAY TO ENJOY CREATION THAN WITH THE CREATOR.

62

COMMIT TO SPIRITUAL GROWTH.

---

ike newborn babies, crave pure
spiritual milk, so that
by it you may grow up in your
salvation, now that you have
tasted that the Lord is good.

1 PETER 2:2-3

When we have a vital and growing relationship with God, it's usually easier to have vital and growing relationships with others. The Bible gives us wisdom, comfort, and guidance for life's bumpy roads. The more we fill our minds and hearts with God's words, the more secure we become as human beings. This also affects our relationships with others—we feel more like reaching out to others when we feel secure within.

Some practical ways to grow spiritually and keep your faith live include: attending church and Sunday school, attending a Bible study, reading good books, and listening to teaching tapes and Christian music. When you feed your soul, you can't help but grow. And when you grow, you'll find your friendships and family relationships growing too.

INVEST IN YOUR SOUL AND SHARE THE DIVIDENDS WITH OTHERS.

63

KEEP YOUR PROMISES TO HIM.

---

*We must not promise what
we ought not, lest we
be called to perform what we cannot.*

Have you ever promised God you would do something—or stop doing something—then later forgot about the promise or brushed it aside? Promises to a holy God shouldn't be taken lightly. Unkept promises create walls between us and our Creator because we lose our confidence to approach Him, and we draw back from His love and blessing.

Think through your vows to God very carefully before making them. When you promise Him something, keep your promise. When you have learned to honor God in this way, you will find it much easier to keep your promises to the earth dwellers in your life. A heart faithful to keep promises made to God will grow a faith that is like a lighthouse to others, always shining in a dark world.

YOUR RELATIONSHIP WITH GOD SHOULD BE BUILT ON PROMISES, NOT COMPROMISES.

64

TRULY WORSHIP HIM.

Worship is transcendent wonder.

True worship isn't about religious rituals, but rather the pure and genuine expression of praise from a willing and eager heart. Children have much to teach us in this regard. Especially when they are young, they come to us without agendas, without pretension, and without motives. They come with true hearts. It is close to impossible to walk away untouched by these unfettered affirmations, and God finds our true worship equally as compelling.

Choose any method you like to worship God: singing, reading Scripture, praying aloud, or by simple and silent reverence—there are a limitless number of ways. No matter how you choose to go about it, remember to do so with the heartlike wonder of a child. Honest, heartfelt worship draws you near to God and increases your trust in His power and love for you.

WORSHIP IS TO THE CHRISTIAN LIFE WHAT THE MAINSPRING IS TO A WATCH.

65

REMEMBER THAT GOD LOVES
ALL HIS CHILDREN.

"He causes his sun to rise on the evil and the good, and sends rain on the righteous and the unrighteous. If you love those who love you, what reward will you get? Are not even the tax collectors doing that?"

MATTHEW 5:45-46

It might be easy to believe that God loves you or Billy Graham or some other great leader, but what about that frightful-looking rock star, dishonest politician, or evil dictator? Do you tend to believe that God must love you more than them?

God loves all His children, though He grieves over those who choose not to respond to His love and care. So the next time you see someone who is offensive to you, remember: God loves that person no less than He loves you or even Jesus, His Son. If you want to keep your faith alive and grow closer to God, you must learn to love the unlovely with the same love He holds in His heart for them.

GOD'S HAND IS EXTENDED
TO ALL MANKIND.

66

REMEMBER THAT MONEY AND MATERIAL GOODS ARE IMMATERIAL.

Money has never yet made anyone rich.

It's ironic that money carries the words "In God We Trust," because wealth—or the pursuit of it—can hinder our trust in God. Money and possessions can never truly satisfy the human soul. A guy named Solomon tried that route and was left empty.

Only God can establish your self-worth and fulfill your deepest longings. Only a relationship with Him can make you alive to His love, aware of your life's purpose, and fill you with inner peace. And unlike money, God will never disappear, be taken away, or lose His value. Remember that money may rule the world's economy, but it takes a backseat in the economy of the kingdom of God.

REMEMBER, IT'S "IN GOD WE TRUST," NOT "IN GOLD WE TRUST."

67

USE YOUR TALENTS.

A bilities are like tax deductions—
we either use them
or we lose them.

God has given everyone abilities. If you develop your skills, you can then use them in a way that will benefit others and bring glory to God. What about your skills? Are you using them? Or are they lying dormant, gathering dust?

Putting your God-given talents to work is one of the most satisfying things you can do. As you do what God created you to do, you gain a deep sense of purpose—and you become closer and more grateful to the One who gave those talents to you. There are few things as beautiful as Creator and creation working hand in hand. So take God's hand, and take some risks. Find your life's purpose, and use everything you've got to serve God in it. The adventure of a life well-lived will keep your faith burning bright.

DO THE BEST THAT YOU CAN DO WITH WHAT YOU ARE GIVEN.

68

BE WILLING TO SEARCH FOR HIM.

We saw his star in the east and have come to worship him.

MATTHEW 2:2

The wise men's friends must have questioned if they were really wise. Here were these fellows, following only hearsay and one bright star on a long journey—a journey filled with unanswered questions and many risks. But their long search was rewarded when they found the Child King, offered their gifts, and expressed their deep and humble adoration.

Even today, the wise men remain examples. Their story can be your story. Are you willing to take the journey—whether physical, intellectual, or spiritual—that will lead you into God's presence? If you are, your faith will receive a workout and you will be rewarded as they were—You will find Him.

WE MAY NO LONGER RIDE CAMELS, BUT WISE MEN AND WOMEN STILL SEEK HIM.

69

LISTEN TO CHRISTIAN MUSIC.

he LORD is my strength

and my song.

PSALM 118:14

Today's Christian music offers something for every taste—from classical to hip-hop to heavy metal. But regardless of their musical style, Christian artists have a common purpose: to glorify God through their music, to proclaim Him to the world, to celebrate life, and to share some of their most honest moments before God. Some artists have revealed that when they are recording, they feel a deep and real sense of God's presence. Small wonder that prophets in the Old Testament sometimes used music to help them hear God's voice.

You can experience His presence as you listen to Christian music today. Visit a music store or Christian bookstore, and choose something in harmony with your own personal taste. And then, take some time to sit back and listen and let your soul soar!

CHRISTIAN MUSIC IS A POWERFUL FORCE THAT CAN BRING US INTO HARMONY WITH GOD.

70

CELEBRATE YOUR INDIVIDUALITY.

---

hank God for the way He made you.
You are special, distinct,
and unique. You were not made
from a common mold.

God didn't make you like anyone else on the entire planet. Even identical twins aren't truly identical. God made you unique, and He has unique plans for you and your talents—and even your limitations.

That's why you must never put yourself down when you are not like everyone else. Instead, revel in your individuality, and thank your Creator who had the inspiration and foresight to make you exactly the way you are. You are special because He has made you so. So look at yourself carefully with God's eyes, and learn what He has in mind for you with your special abilities, likes, and dislikes. Understanding your individual purpose will liven up your faith and draw you closer to Him.

YOU WERE FEARFULLY AND WONDERFULLY FORMED IN YOUR MOTHER'S WOMB, NOT MASS-PRODUCED ON AN ASSEMBLY LINE.

71

LEARN THAT LESS IS MORE.

---

*If I cannot do great things,
I can do small things
in a great way.*

It is commonly thought that bigger is better. Our world loves bigness. Large, economy-sized boxes of detergent. Supersized meals. Vehicles with extra leg- and headroom. God often does things on a grand scale as well. He parted the Red Sea, and He created the universe in less than a week.

But sometimes less is more. God used only a small army to defeat the mighty Midianites and fed a whole multitude of people from one boy's small lunch. And most importantly, He sent a tiny baby to save the world.

Don't measure your success by how big your possessions are or how big you are in the eyes of others. God isn't impressed with your bigness. He is interested in your life and the small but faithful steps you take toward Him each day.

LITTLE THINGS MAKE A
BIG DIFFERENCE TO GOD.

72

REMEMBER THAT YOU DON'T
LOOK GOOD IN GREEN.

---

*Envy takes the joy, happiness, and
contentment out of living.*

God hates jealousy so much that He addressed the issue in the Ten Commandments: You shall not covet. We are all God's creation. He loves us all, and we needn't compare our blessings with those of others. When we envy what others have, we rob ourselves of the joy and contentment we could be finding in the good things God has already given us.

In your efforts to grow your faith, guard your heart. If you find that you are unable to rejoice over the success of others, beware. Instead of focusing on what others have, ask God to remind you of the many blessings He has given you—and how many of them are undeserved. Discipline yourself to thank God for the blessings of others and to pray that He will continue to bless them.

GOD'S CHILDREN SHOULD BE ZEALOUS, NOT JEALOUS.

73

LEARN GOD'S WILL
THROUGH HIS WORD.

---

*This is the confidence we have in approaching
God: that if we ask anything
according to his will, he hears us.
And if we know that he hears us—
whatever we ask—we know that
we have what we asked of him.*

1 JOHN 5:14-15

God is not Santa Claus, nor is He a heavenly vending machine. But He does want to shower you with blessings. There is a prerequisite, however. To receive a yes answer to a request you present to God in prayer, you must ask for those things that are in line with His will. Thankfully, He has not left it up to us to guess what His will is. His will is His Word—the Bible—and it is filled with hundreds of promises He has made to you. He wants to say yes to you, and He will do just that, when you pray according to His will.

So the next time you have a need or desire something of your Heavenly Father, search the Bible for promises related to that request, and then present your requests to Him. If you have God's word on your request, then don't give up hope when He seems to take some time in answering. He will answer you. And when He says yes, don't forget to thank Him.

GOD DELIGHTS IN SAYING
YES TO YOUR PRAYERS.

74

STAND ON THE RIGHT FOUNDATION.

---

*Now faith is being sure of
what we hope for
and certain of what we do not see.*

HEBREWS 11:1

Emotions are wonderful. They add flavor and spice to life. They make us feel more alive. They make life more fun. Emotions, however, make a lousy foundation for our faith in God because they can be radically affected by things such as diet, lack of sleep, and internal chemistry, not to mention the weather. You should never look to your feelings to judge whether or not God loves You. His Word already promises that He is crazy about you! Besides, if you rely on goose bumps or chills running down your spine as proof of God's love, it could be the flu that is causing it!

Thank God that His love for us isn't based on how we *feel;* it's based on His integrity. His promises are true, regardless of how we feel. Standing on the fact that God's love is always there for you can help you when feelings move in the opposite direction to that truth, and you feel as if your faith is taking a hit.

GOD'S LOVE IS MORE THAN A FEELING; IT'S A FACT.

75

REMEMBER THAT YOU ARE
PART OF HIS RELAY TEAM.

We have received the baton of faith.
We must pass it carefully
on to the next generation.

Just as you benefit from the encouragement of believers who have gone before you, you must run your leg of the race too, then pass your story of faith on to others. Many cultures are known for their rich oral tradition. In fact, much of the Bible is just that—a faithful retelling of God's impact on the events and lives of those who have served Him. Think of where we would be if no one before us had shared their stories of faith!

Be sure and do your part. Tell your friends about your "God events." Tell your family. Write down the times when God speaks to you or teaches you something, and keep it collected in a journal to share with your kids and grandkids. Yes, yours is only one of many stories, but it is real and it is worth preserving.

DON'T FORGET TO KEEP THE MEMORY OF GOD ALIVE.

76

GO TO HIM IN TIMES OF TROUBLE.

God is our refuge and strength,

a very present

help in trouble.

PSALM 46:1 KJV

Some of the closest relationships are forged in times of crisis—on the battlefield, in the hospital, or during a natural disaster. Yet many people run from God—out of anger or despair—when calamity occurs, forfeiting a wonderful opportunity to grow closer to Him.

If you're tempted to flee from God in times of trouble, know that He never loses control of any situation. He knows what He is doing, and He is aware of everything that is happening. So when trouble strikes, don't leave His protection. Remember, He promises that if you come close to Him, He will come close to you. Cling to Him with your whole heart, and stay full of faith, knowing He will take care of you.

WHEN YOU FACE TROUBLE, GO TO GOD ON THE DOUBLE.

77

MOVE PAST FAILURES.

The greatest failure is the failure to try.

As imperfect people, we make mistakes. We drop the ball, miss the mark, fall on our faces, use too many clichés. Failure can make us feel inadequate, especially when we compare ourselves to others who seem to be living more effectively.

When you feel like a failure, especially when you compare yourself to others, remember the focal point of your life: You have chosen to live in close fellowship with God out of your love for Him rather than to impress an audience of your peers. Focus on God, and know that He will cheer you on—and pick you up and dust you off when you fall. He won't hold your failures against you, so don't hold them against yourself.

TRY AGAIN. GOD IS NOT AS WORRIED ABOUT YOUR FAILURES AS YOU ARE.

78

WELCOME ADVERSITY.

Adversity can either destroy or build up, depending on our chosen response.

When athletes train hard, they run or lift weights to the point of muscle failure. This approach actually breaks down muscle fibers, which would seem to be detrimental to performance. However, it's beneficial because the body adapts to the stress and rebuilds the damaged fibers stronger than ever before.

This principle is also important to our spiritual strength and stamina. God does not cause our pain and struggle, but a certain amount of adversity inevitably will come into our lives. He desires to see that we grow strong and resilient rather than weak and complacent. So smile when you encounter trials, even if others think you are insane to do so. See your difficulties as opportunities to grow strong in your faith and closer to God— that is exactly how He sees them.

DON'T BE GUILTY OF GIVING TRIALS AN UNJUST VERDICT.

79

PUT AWAY YOUR GAVEL.

"Do not judge, or you too will be judged."

MATTHEW 7:1

Judges today are celebrities. Some even have their own television shows where they scold, cajole, and sentence those who come before them. Sometimes it's tempting to put on the long black robes ourselves and pass judgment on others. It's easy for us to see their faults and pronounce them guilty. There's only one problem. In the kingdom of God, being judgmental is courting disaster.

When you pronounce verdicts on others, you open yourself up to the same kind of prosecution from them and from God. Not only that, but often we judge in others the very faults we suffer from ourselves, leaving us no room for mercy that we definitely need. So leave the judging to God. And when you see others misbehaving, pray for them, and thank God for His mercy, which is available to all, including you when you need it—mercy that is free for the asking.

SITTING HIGH IN THE JUDGMENT SEAT KEEPS YOU FROM GETTING ON YOUR KNEES.

80

LOOK IN THE MIRROR AND SAY, "HELLO, MASTERPIECE."

God created man in his own image, in the image of God he created him; male and female he created them.

GENESIS 1:27

Ephesians 2:10 tells us that we are "God's workmanship, created in Christ Jesus to do good works." That means we are God's works of art. Imagine that. You are the creation of the only perfect artist that ever has been or ever will be. And the news just keeps getting better. God didn't craft you merely to sit around collecting dust in some cosmic art gallery. He created you for a purpose—His purpose.

So next time your self-esteem takes a hit, and you think you aren't important enough, smart enough, sophisticated enough, charming enough, rich enough, or good-looking enough to be of any use to God, remember who you are—God's work of art. God's *functional* work of art. And remember also that there are tasks He has planned for you that only you can do. God has designed you in such a way that the world needs what you can do.

GOD'S WORKS OF ART ARE BUILT FOR ACTION, NOT AUCTION.

81

GROW IN YOUR KNOWLEDGE OF GOD.

Oh, the depth of the riches of the wisdom
and knowledge of God!
How unsearchable his judgments,
and his paths beyond tracing out!
"Who has known the mind of the Lord?
Or who has been his counselor?"

ROMANS 11:33-34

Many people like to reduce God to something small and simple enough for their finite minds to grasp. They want to put God into a nice, neat little box. But God's ways are not our ways. He is infinite, and we are human, subject to human limitations. As long as we are on this earth, we can grow in our knowledge about God, and we can even know Him personally. But we won't fully comprehend His glory until we meet Him face to face. Then "we shall see him as he is" (1 John 3:2).

A clear understanding of God cannot be obtained by intellectual pursuit. It must be a venture of the heart, received by faith. So relax, and quit trying to figure Him out. But do spend quality time with Him, listening to Him and to His Word. Let Him reveal to you what He wants you to know about Him. In this way you can just enjoy getting to know Him and receive His bountiful love.

KNOWING GOD IS A MATTER OF THE HEART, NOT THE HEAD.

82

FLY WITH EAGLES RATHER THAN CRAWL WITH SLUGS.

He who walks with the wise grows wise, but a companion of fools suffers harm.

PROVERBS 13:20

Companionship choices are difficult. Jesus spent time with many people with low reputation. Yet the Bible cautions us that bad company corrupts good character. The key to following Jesus' example *and* protecting ourselves lies in discernment. Follow these simple guidelines.

First, spend as much time as possible with God and with godly people who will encourage you to keep your faith alive by growing closer to Him. Second, as you befriend troubled people, be careful to do so on *your* terms, as much as possible. This means that you choose the location, any other participants, and the activity whenever you can. And third, you must constantly ask yourself, *Am I drawing these people toward God, or are they drawing me away?*

KEEP IN MIND THAT IT'S EASIER TO BE PULLED DOWN THAN TO BE PULLED UP.

83

SHARE HIS FEELINGS.

Before we can feel the deepest tenderness for others, we must feel the deepest tenderness of God.

The Bible says that God has intense feelings—sorrow over those who reject His love, compassion for those who are hurting, joy over those who turn from their destructive ways.

As with any relationship, when emotions are shared, a special bond forms. You feel what the other feels, and your hearts are knit together. Why would our relationship with God be any different? He wants us to be moved by what moves Him, to love others as He loves them. Yet He is also touched by those things that touch us.

Today, ask Him to help you feel what He feels, to see others as He sees them. Perhaps He might even use you to meet another's need. In doing so you will find that your faith in Him will increase, and your love for Him will grow by leaps and bounds!

SHARED FEELINGS
PROMOTE INTIMACY.

84

GO TO CHURCH.

Let us not give up meeting together.

HEBREWS 10:25

If you are serious about your relationship with God and nurturing your faith in Him, then it is vitally important that you find a church home where you feel comfortable and attend regularly. Meeting together with other believers provides encouragement and instruction as you walk the road of faith. And God loves it when His people gather together to enjoy each other's company and worship Him together. After all, if you are one of His favorite people, doesn't it stand to reason that He would want to share you with His other favorites?

Once you find the right congregation, take time to get to know those you see every week. Take time to learn about the services and programs your church can provide. Get involved with the activities your church provides for church members and the community as a whole. You will be blessed by the support and comfort a church family can provide.

SORROWS ARE DIMINISHED AND JOYS MULTIPLIED WHEN YOU SHARE THEM.

85

RESPOND IMMEDIATELY
TO HIS CALLING.

What I mean, brothers, is that the time is short.

1 CORINTHIANS 7:29

The Bible tells us to redeem the time (Ephesians 5:16 KJV). That means that we should make the most of every opportunity, because some opportunities don't linger for long. So when we feel a prompting from our Heavenly Father, we should never say, "Leave a message, and I'll get back to You later." Remember, God has legions of angels who will do whatever He asks. How much more should we—His children, created in His image and after His likeness—be quick to obey.

It's our loss when we miss the opportunity to serve Him, because even when we do things for Him that are difficult or unpleasant, there is a reward that comes as a special joy from working with Him. That experience increases your faith and your eagerness to serve the next time He calls. Respond immediately when you hear God speak. His will is wonderful, and His plans for you always lead to abundant life.

THE TIME YOU KILL CAN NEVER BE RESUSCITATED.

86

REALIZE THERE IS NOWHERE
HE WON'T GO.

---

*If the Lord be with us, we have no
cause of fear. His eye is upon us,
His arm over us, His ear open
to our prayer—His grace sufficient,
His promise unchangeable.*

"Don't go there" is one of the most overused phrases of the late 1990s. But it doesn't apply to God. He never sends His children anywhere alone. In Old Testament times, He was with them as a pillar of fire, a cloud, a burning bush, and a voice from Heaven. Today, He is with us in the form of His Holy Spirit, the Bible, as well as godly leaders and friends.

So, if you're enduring trials, be encouraged by the thought that He is with you, and remember that the Lord has gone before you and knows ahead of time what you need. He knows what must be done in each case, either to lift the trial or to strengthen you to bear up under it and come through a victor.

REST IN THE KNOWLEDGE THAT THERE IS NOWHERE YOU CAN GO THAT GOD CANNOT REACH.

87

MEDITATE ON HIS WORD.

A man of meditation is happy,
not for an hour or a day,
but quite round the circle
of all his years.

Some people are frightened by the word *meditation*. It evokes images of bearded gurus sitting cross-legged in robes and chanting meaningless monosyllables. However, to meditate simply means to think deeply and continuously about something. If you can worry over something, you will meditate like a champion.

For the person who wants to nurture their faith, meditation can consist merely of focusing on the Bible's teachings and the God behind them. You "talk" to yourself about a verse or a truth and try to see it from all the directions you can think of. When you meditate, God comes to you and suggests ideas and thoughts that give you new insights into God's mind and His world. Choose an appropriate verse and meditate on God's goodness, on His wisdom and counsel, on His love and kindness. Meditate on His awesome creation and wondrous works. It doesn't matter what aspect of God you choose, meditating on Him and His Word will transform your life.

DON'T HESITATE
TO MEDITATE.

88

DEDICATE YOUR EFFORTS TO HIM.

Serve wholeheartedly, as if you were

serving the Lord, not men, because

you know that the Lord will reward

everyone for whatever good he does.

EPHESIANS 6:7-8

Legendary college football coach Knute Rockne gleaned a marvelous performance from his team one time by urging them to "win one for the Gipper," a deceased former player. How much more motivation can we muster by dedicating our efforts to Jesus who died for us and now lives for us, as well as to the God who created us and loves us eternally?

Whether you're doing something athletic, artistic, or career-oriented, do it for God. Dedicate everything you do to God as a gesture of appreciation for the talents He has placed in your life. Then, however your efforts turn out, you will know the joy of pleasing and honoring Him.

GIVE IT ALL YOU'VE GOT FOR GOD.

89

REMEMBER.

---

*When memory makes a journey into
the past we live not once,
but twice, the best times of our lives.*

"You're only as good as your last game" is a popular adage in sports today. And a hit song a few years ago asked the question, "What have you done for me lately?" Look at the story of the Israelites in the Old Testament. They forgot about how God had parted the Red Sea and delivered them from their oppressors. Soon after that miraculous event, they forgot Him and worshipped a golden statue of a calf as their deliverer!

It's important to remember all God has done for you—all the love, mercy, and answered prayers that have brought you to this point in your life. So write down those important faith events in the back of your Bible or in a journal. That same God will be with you in the future, but never forget what He's done in the past. An attitude of remembrance keeps your faith alive.

TOO MANY PEOPLE HAVE SHORT MEMORIES AND LONG LISTS OF WANTS.

90

CONCENTRATE ON BEING
FAITHFUL, NOT SUCCESSFUL.

"*Well done, good and faithful servant!*
You have been faithful with
a few things; I will put you in charge
of many things. Come and share
your master's happiness!"

MATTHEW 25:21

In contemporary society, people are judged by numbers—
how much money they grossed last year, how many new clients
they brought in, how many "toys" they have. Given the world's
view of success, it's easy to assume that God thinks the same way.
Thus, people sometimes focus on church attendance, number of
volunteer activities, or the amount of money they put into the
offering as the ways to please Him.

God is not some great statistician in the sky. He's more
concerned with the state of your heart than how many good
deeds you perform. So focus on simply being faithful to Him.
Spend time with Him, learn His ways, and become someone who
knows what His passions are. Do this, and success will take care
of itself.

IF AT FIRST YOU DON'T SUCCEED, BE FAITHFUL AND KEEP TRYING.

91

BE UNAFRAID OF AGE.

*It's not how old you are,
but how you are old.*

Vitamins. Nutritional supplements. Mud packs. Face creams. Face-lifts. Miracle diets. America is obsessed with fighting old age. And with good reason—some people fear aging more than they fear an IRS audit or even death itself.

Yet age is not an enemy to you as a child of God. Although your earthly body is aging, inwardly you are being renewed day by day (2 Corinthians 4:16). You are on a pilgrimage that will lead you to a heavenly home where you will have a wonderful new body. Your spirit, the real you that will dwell in that new body, is eternal. So instead of focusing on reversing the aging process in your old body, concentrate on growing spiritually by renewing your mind with God's Word. Give yourself a "spirit lift," a true renewal, by spending time with God and basking in the warmth of His love.

THERE'S NO NEED TO FEAR OLD AGE WHEN YOU'VE RECEIVED THE NEW BIRTH.

92

BE HONEST WITH GOD.

Trust in Him at all times, O people;

Pour out your heart

before Him; God is a refuge for us.

PSALM 62:8 NASB

Sometimes you can be tempted to run away from God and to blame Him for not protecting you from trouble or for allowing disaster to fall upon you. But go directly to God and tell Him exactly how you feel. Tell Him about your anger with Him, your disappointment that He didn't do as you thought He should. Cry, stomp, yell—but don't walk away.

If you don't feel comfortable yelling, go to Psalms, or read Job in a modern translation. Here were believers in trouble, and they had the courage to stay with God and work it out. David prayed with raw honesty, and yet he moved to a position of faith at the same time. Job was a daredevil with his anger and honesty, yet God loved him and blessed him. You be honest too. Pour your heart out before Him. He can take it, and your faith will grow in your wrestling with Him.

GOD CAN TAKE
YOUR HONESTY.

93

BE ANXIOUS FOR NOTHING.

Worry is the misuse of the imagination.

In Philippians 4:6, Paul instructs us to "be anxious for *nothing.*" Think about that. Paul says the child of God shouldn't worry about anything at all! And Paul didn't give this advice lightly. He was in prison at the time he wrote those words. But despite all his trials, Paul knew God would take care of him and give him the grace he needed. God doesn't always untie all the knots in our lives. But He does give us the grace to live with them.

So remember, there is nothing you face that is too difficult, too troubling, or too frightening for God. He holds the world in the palm of His hand. Your problems aren't likely to stump Him. Allow news like that to pump up your faith!

TURN YOUR WORRIES OVER TO GOD, AND LET HIS PERFECT PEACE SETTLE YOUR HEART.

94

LISTEN TO HIM.

" *My sheep listen to my voice;
I know them,
and they follow me.*"

JOHN 10:27

Communication is vital to any relationsip, and listening is key. God listens to us, and we must listen to Him if the relationship is to be meaningful. You may hear Him through a Scripture passage, a sermon, a song, even through the words of a child. Like tuning into your favorite radio station, we must tune our ears to hear what He is saying.

Ask Him to give you hearing ears, then keep your spiritual antenna up, expecting to hear what He has to say. You may receive an impression in your heart or a strong knowing on the inside. As you practice listening, you'll begin to perceive His voice more and more, and your relationship with Him will enter new depths. Your trust in Him will grow because you will get to know Him and will be more and more certain of His goodness. So sit still each day for some minutes just to listen.

WHAT IS HE SAYING TO YOU?

95

LAUGH AT YOURSELF.

A cheerful heart is a good medicine.

PROVERBS 17:22 NRSV

In general, laughter promotes good health, both in body and spirit. It not only brightens your mood but also eases tension. A good dose of laughter has been shown to improve blood circulation, stimulate digestion, lower blood pressure, and prompt the brain to release pain-reducing endorphins.

However, laughter is also an expression of faith in God—you can laugh at yourself, because you know God isn't through with you yet. Sometimes it is the best response you can make to your own human frailties as you grow in your life of faith. Mistakes are inevitable as you grow, but you can weather them if you put them in their proper perspective, the way we do when little children make mistakes as they learn to walk and talk.

DO SOMETHING FOR YOUR HEALTH TODAY—LAUGH!

96

BEGIN AND END EACH DAY WITH GENUINE THANKSGIVING TO GOD.

---

*Enter into his gates with thanksgiving,
and into his courts with praise:
be thankful unto him, and bless his name.*

PSALM 100:4 KJV

Nothing enhances your faith more than acknowledging the good things in your life and thanking God for them. Even when your circumstances are grim, you can always find something to be thankful for. Why is this important? Human nature causes us to focus on the negative, and the negative overwhelms our inner sense of contentment, putting a damper on our walk of faith.

Rehearsing the positive aspects of your life will help you restore a delicate emotional balance and stabilize your inner compass. There is no better way to gain perspective and jump-start your faith than to begin your day and end it with a time when you remember all that God is doing, all that He has done, and all that He is as He gives himself to you.

COUNT YOUR BLESSINGS EVERY MORNING, AND THANK GOD FOR THEM ONE BY ONE!

97

CONSISTENTLY CULTIVATE
TIMES OF SOLITUDE.

*Alone with God! It is there that
what is hid with God is made known
—God's ideals, God's hopes, God's doings.*

As a vessel takes shape on a potter's wheel, the potter applies pressure to both the inside and the outside of the pot as it spins. Without the inside pressure, the pot would collapse inward. Without the outside pressure, the pot would not retain any shape. But both pressures need to be in the right proportion to each other.

Human beings need strength coming from the inside to withstand the everyday pressures exerted from the outside. When we spend regular time in quiet solitude, listening to the heartbeat of God, we are strengthened from within and become more in tune with Him. Spending time alone with God will keep life from crushing us and will result in a life whose shape demonstrates what God can do.

EVEN IN SOLITUDE,
YOU ARE NEVER ALONE.
GOD IS WITH YOU.

98

LOOK AT LIFE IN THE LIGHT OF GOD'S LOVE.

*The voyage of discovery lies not in
finding new landscapes,
but in having new eyes.*

In a meditation on the love of God written in the fourteenth century, Julian of Norwich wrote that God called her attention to a hazelnut she was holding in the palm of her hand. She marveled at it, so small, seemingly so insignificant, and yet suddenly valuable beyond measure because God had created it, had a purpose for it, and loved it. She concluded, "Everything owes its existence to the love of God."

Life is filled with these manifestations of God's infinite care. Open your eyes to see, and you, too, can experience the happiness of knowing that you are not just valued by the Creator of the universe—you are loved by the same Creator who delights in you and smiles when He thinks of you!.

WHEN WE TRULY STOP TO
SEE WHAT GOD HAS MADE
FOR US TO ENJOY, WE FIND
HIS LOVE AT EVERY TURN.

99

REMEMBER THAT HEAVEN
IS A REAL PLACE.

The world has forgotten,
in its concern with Left and Right,

that there is an Above and Below.

A young man completing a job application came to the line asking for his permanent address. He thought for a moment, then wrote, "Heaven." He understood that Heaven is a real place—and ultimately, it will be his home and the home of all those who put their trust in Jesus Christ.

One way to become more conscious of Him in your everyday life is to remember that Jesus has gone ahead of you to prepare a special place just for you. Someday you will actually meet Him face-to-face! Look forward to it with eager anticipation as you would an upcoming vacation, and realize that Heaven will be far more wonderful than even the most fantastic earthly destination. Even better, you will never have to leave. Heaven is your permanent address—rest your faith on that.

WHAT'S AHEAD OF US
IS FAR BETTER THAN
ANYTHING THAT'S BEHIND US.

100

SEEK THE UNITY JESUS PRAYED FOR.

We must learn to live together like brothers or we will perish together like fools.

Jesus fervently prayed to God that believers "be brought to complete unity to let the world know that you sent me . . ." (John 17:23). Unfortunately, there are many things that hinder unity. Racism, for example, breeds hatred and misunderstanding and undermines the spiritual lives of believers.

Imagine what God thinks when some of the people He has created think they are better than others simply because of skin color. Pray for racial harmony and pursue relationships with people of different races and backgrounds. As you do this, you will be part of the answer to Jesus' prayer, and you can be sure that the heart of the God who plays no favorites will be with you.

TO GOD, THERE IS
ONLY ONE RACE:
THE HUMAN RACE.

101

USE YOUR WORDS WISELY.

---

*The tongue has the power
of life and death,
and those who love it
will eat its fruit.*

PROVERBS 18:21

Words are a powerful form of communication. Not only are words important, *but* how we say them is just as important. Observe the impact that your words have on others. Listen for the inflections you use. Try to become aware of your facial expressions and body language as you communicate.

The apostle Paul admonished us to always have our conversation be full of grace. The virtuous woman of Proverbs 31 has the law of kindness on her lips. Even more, the words that come out of your mouth can lift the spirits of the discouraged, move the hearts of the insensitive, and catch the imagination of the young. You can change the world without leaving your hometown merely by choosing your words carefully and prayerfully!

YOU CAN CHANGE THE WORLD
WITH YOUR WORDS.

ACKNOWLEDGEMENTS

(8) Thomas Merton, (12) Agnes Miegel, (16, 80, 154) Taylor Morgan, (18) American Proverb, (24) Walt Whitman, (30) Elizabeth Barrett Browning, (36) Zig Ziglar, (38) St. Francis of Assisi, (42, 62) Chinese Proverb, (44) William Stoughton, (54) Cecil Myers, (56, 130) Abraham Lincoln, (64) Henry Ward Beecher, (66) Leo Tolstoy, (68) T.J. Bower, (76) Victor Hugo, (78) John Wesley, (84) Mark Lowry, (90) Olivia Kent, (104) Charles H. Spurgeon, (106) Brooks Atkinson, (114) Drew Cody, (122) Michel Quoist, (126) Richard W. Langer, (132) Thomas Carlyle, (136) Seneca, (138) Sam Jennings, (144) Erwin W. Lutzer, (146) James Freeman Clarke, (148) Billy Graham, (158) William Ward, (160) Tim Hansel, (170) Emily Morgan, (176) John Newton, (178) Isaac Taylor, (182) E.C. Rayburn, (186) Marie Dressler, (190) Author Unknown, (198) Oswald Chambers, (200) Marcel Proust, (202) Glen Drake, (204) Martin Luther King Jr.

Additional copies of this book
are available from your local bookstore.

The following titles are also available
in this series:
101 Simple Secrets to Keep Your Hope Alive
101 Simple Secrets to Keep Your Love Alive

If you have enjoyed this book,
or if it has impacted your life,
we would like to hear from you.
Please contact us at:
Honor Books
An Imprint of Cook Communications Ministries
4050 Lee Vance View
Colorado Springs, CO 80918
www.cookministries.com